What people are saying about *Weird Christians*...

In his book *Weird Christians I Have Met*, Phil Baker is nonjudgmental but entertaining and insightful in pointing out the extreme viewpoints of various groups of Christians and why we must move toward balance to be effective. It was great fun to read and a little embarrassing to see shades of myself in my earlier Christian development.

If you've been a Christian for a few years, you've met most of the weird characters Phil Baker analyzes.

Phil, your dry wit and humor always refresh me!

—*Rick Godwin*
Senior Pastor, Hillsong Church
Sydney, Australia

Church life has always been colored by its great diversity of characters, and this book paints an amusing picture of some of the Christian stereotypes we have all encountered (or possibly once were!). Phil's witty style and clever character sketches are not only an entertaining read, but his perceptive observations reveal the great need for balance in our Christian walk.

—*Brian Houston*
Senior Pastor, Hillsong Church
Sydney, Australia

In his unique style, Phil Baker has given us a humorous and insightful look at Christianity in his book *Weird Christians I Have Met*. Phil is a brilliant communicator with a message worth hearing. I highly recommend this book.

—*Bayless Conley*
Senior Pastor, Cottonwood Christian Center
Los Alamitos, California

These pages offer the voice of Philip Baker, a person of modern sensibility with revealing insights into our idiosyncratic ways. Lucid, luminous, and logical.

—J. John
International Evangelist and Best-Selling Author

Weird Christians I Have Met is extremely funny, insightful, and challenging. It is a truly great piece of satirical Christian writing from one of Australia's most inspirational Christian leaders. It will challenge all Christians to be balanced, authentic, and normal.

—Rev. Dr. Mark Stibbe
Senior Leader, St. Andrew's Church
International Conference Speaker and Best-Selling Author
Chorleywood, United Kingdom

This book calls us to shun the extreme, the bizarre, and the prejudice that are impediments to the church being an influential force. You may laugh, you may cringe, but you will be challenged. Philip Baker is "out of the box." His thought-provoking style is a call to "rut-free living." *Weird Christians I Have Met* carries Phil's special brand of humor. It's fun with punch.

—Wayne Alcorn
Senior Minister, Brisbane City Church
Brisbane, Australia

Philip Baker's thought-provoking writing style, his sense of humor, and his wonderful gift to teach about life and truth makes this a "must read." You will love it.

—Danny Guglielmucci
Senior Minister, Southside Christian Church
Adelaide, Australia

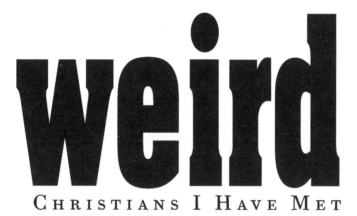

weird

CHRISTIANS I HAVE MET

weird

CHRISTIANS I HAVE MET

PHILIP BAKER

WHITAKER
HOUSE

deepercalling

WEIRD CHRISTIANS I HAVE MET

ISBN-13: 978-0-88368-805-2
ISBN-10: 0-88368-805-0
Printed in the United States of America
Australia: © 1997 Philip Leonard Baker
United States of America: © 2005 Philip Leonard Baker

WHITAKER
HOUSE

1030 Hunt Valley Circle
New Kensington, PA 15068
www.whitakerhouse.com

deepercalling
www.deepercalling.com

Library of Congress Cataloging-in-Publication Data
Baker, Philip (Philip Leonard)
Weird Christians I have met / Philip Baker.
p.   cm.
Summary: "Examines the extremes of Christianity through humorous fictionalized character profiles in an attempt to find balance and authenticity in the Christian life"—Provided by publisher.
ISBN-13: 978-0-88368-805-2 (trade pbk. : alk. paper)
ISBN-10: 0-88368-805-0 (trade pbk. : alk. paper)
1. Christian life—Humor. I. Title.
BV4517.B35 2005
242—dc22   2004028341

1 2 3 4 5 6 7 8 9 10 11 **ᵁᴶ** 12 11 10 09 08 07 06 05

*To
Ed,
Pamela,
Theo,
Dave,
Frank,
Bob,
Garfield,
Jill,
Patricia,
and Pete,
without whose inspiration this book would not
have been possible.*

CONTENTS

PREFACE

In northern England, where I grew up, the locals often said, "There's nowt so queer as folks!" That may need a little translation, so how about, "In a world full of strange phenomena, there is nothing as strange as people." People believe and do strange things. But who decides who is strange and who is normal?

Philip Baker, senior pastor of one of the largest churches in Australia, is concerned enough to answer these questions and, given his long pastoral experience, keen insights, and generous spirit, he is well qualified for the task. Mercifully, he is also blessed with a keen sense of humor, which means he writes about issues that could easily raise hackles, but instead he manages to generate chuckles.

This does not mean that he treats serious issues lightly or trivializes fervently held positions. What it does mean is that he has written a book that is easily read, gently challenging, and potentially beneficial to all who, like him, want to see God's people "keeping the main things the main things."

—Stuart Briscoe
Minister-at-Large, Elmbrook Church, Brookfield, WI
Best-Selling Author of *Secrets of Spiritual Stamina,*
The Apostles' Creed: Beliefs That Matter, and
Choices for a Lifetime: Determining the Values That
Will Shape Your Future

Weird
Christians
I
Have
Met

WHY
AREN'T
YOU
NORMAL
LIKE
ME?

all things weird and wonderful

Is committing one's life to Christ also a commitment to a loss of identity and individuality? After all, don't Christians all look alike, dress alike, and smile nicely at one another in between choruses of "I love you with the love of the Lord"? I don't think so! Yet such fear and false perception can be major obstacles for the seeking soul.

Perception becomes reality, and fear frustrates faith, especially if one believes that walking with God causes the sparkle and unpredictability of life to be lost. So, for many, their ideas of Christianity and church are filled with boredom or even revulsion. We need panache not predictability, creativity not clones, life not liturgy. Faith is meant to be vital, and church is meant to be thrilling. As we begin to look deeper into these matters, we find that, indeed, they are.

One soon discovers that the great strength of the Christian church is its diversity. Although there are some who would like to push us all toward the clonism (that's a new word!) of Christians, I personally delight in the plethora of polychromatic personalities that one discovers within the body of Christ.

There are all sorts of believers. There are fat ones, thin ones, liberal and conservative ones, left-wing and right-wing, yuppie and grunge, boring and bizarre. Within the Christian world there are fans of both Monty Python and *The Cosby Show*, fans of George Michael and Kenny Rogers.

I personally believe that difference is what makes this world, and indeed the church, such an interesting place. I love the fact that within our own church we embrace a host of political, economic, and ethical positions—all within the framework of Christianity. Furthermore, heaven, to me, would not be heaven if one could not choose between sushi and spaghetti, between cappuccino and Coke.

One of the characteristics of a cult is that its teaching of "the truth" necessarily leads to an extremely narrow range of opinions and behaviors. Yet, an encounter with authentic Christianity reveals that depth and variety are not enemies to be scorned but friends to be embraced.

Depth and variety are not enemies to be scorned

God gave us diverse personalities, wired us in a multitude of ways, and distributed among us many kinds of gifts. The simple and the scholarly, the gentle carer and the strong leader, all have their place in God's economy.

A few years back there was a push among some to demonize denominations. "There is only one church," was the cry. "Difference is of the Devil."

Let the reader understand: I am wholeheartedly for unity within the church. The sooner we realize that what holds us together is far stronger than what tries to separate us, the better. In our city of Perth, Western Australia, over one hundred and forty churches of different denominations gather each year in an annual event called The Church Together, which now attracts up to fifteen thousand people. The clear message gained from this type of meeting is that most Christians, while reveling in the excitement of their own meetings, are happy to meet in churches with different backgrounds.

We are not to denigrate the church down the road because its worship style or theological emphasis is different from our own. We must realize that not all people have our needs, background, Christian culture, or personality and that to reach all types of people, we need all types of churches and denominations.

The ability to appreciate those who are different from ourselves is one of the attributes of mature Christianity. There is, however, a ditch on both sides of this particular road. On the one hand we can try to force everybody into our particular culturally defined, denominationally sanctioned definition of Christian life and practice. Or, on the other hand, we can become so broad and accepting that we nurture an "anything goes" type of approach, where there is no distinction between good and evil, or right and wrong. In the name of tolerance and nonjudgmentalism, we turn the narrow way of which Jesus spoke into a broad park where all are free to roam as they like, with no boundaries, no directions, and no signposts.

There is a subtle balance between normal Christianity, with its appreciation of diversity, and that which is erroneous, misleading, and ultimately damaging. This book is an attempt to navigate these dangerous waters. My hope is that together we will be able to distinguish between the diverse and the dangerous, the wonderful and the weird.

Weird or Normal?

The word *weird* conjures up all sorts of images. It means different things to different people. The word as it is used today means "out of the ordinary, uncanny, abnormal" or, as the Oxford Dictionary puts it, "uncomfortably strange."

Many would use the word to describe all Christians, and indeed, in a sense we should be addressed as "weird." The point is, we are meant to be different from the world. We are a *"peculiar people"* (1 Peter 2:9 KJV); we are salt in a decaying society and light in the midst of great darkness. However, in the context of this book, I am using the word *weird* not in comparison to the world but in comparison to the life of Christ.

In this sense the "normal Christian" is the one who orders his or her behavior as close as possible to the pattern found in the New

Testament and as exemplified by the character of Christ. The "weird Christian" then is one whose lifestyle and direction is radically different from this ideal.

The Christian life seems pretty boring until one attempts to live it

One of the problems we face is that the phrase "the normal Christian life" sounds pretty boring—that is, until one attempts to live it. Only then do we begin to discover that following in the steps of Christ is, as one writer put it, "living tiptoe on the edge of expectation." Many authors have attempted to make this point. C. S. Lewis entitled his analysis and defense of Christianity simply as *Mere Christianity*, while Watchman Nee and John Stott write books with titles such as *The Normal Christian Life* and *Basic Christianity*. The point is that normal, basic, mere Christianity can change our lives, revitalize our communities, and impact our world.

The Means and the End

I have also discovered that one of the best vehicles for truth is satire. In the words of Mary Poppins, "A spoonful of sugar helps the medicine go down." So, with tongue planted firmly in cheek, let us proceed into the crazy world of bizarre Christians where, together, we may run into familiar characters, recognize friends, or even spot ourselves.

In our lighthearted discussion of "weird Christians," we must give them names, and as a result, some are men and some are women. Weirdness, however, is gender free, so for every Pentecostal Pamela there are as many Pentecostal Pauls. And I hear Backslidden Bob is good pals with Backslidden Betty. In short, if there are any Feminist Felicities (or Freds for that matter) reading this, let me assure you I am not picking on men or women, just on weirdness, which is neither male nor female in nature.

The authentic Christian is one of the most attractive and compelling reasons for seeking the truth of Christianity. However, we are often our own worst enemy, for the inauthentic Christian—the overly religious, fanatical, or sidetracked believer—repels the seeking soul. Indeed, the number one reason why many people will not consider the claims of Christ is because they have encountered Christians—or, I should say, "weird Christians."

I trust that *Weird Christians I Have Met* in some way addresses this situation. My purpose in writing is to champion basic Christianity and highlight the dangers of misapplied theology and out of balance believers.

2

END-TIME ED

caught up in the last daze

I once lived next door to an End-Time Ed. Initially, I was quite excited that a fellow Christian was living in close proximity to my apartment, but the "Beware the Mark" bumper sticker on his motorcycle helmet should have alerted me to the fact that our fellowship would be monothematic. Don't get me wrong, End-Time Ed is committed to Christ and to the local church and, like all the weird Christians we will discuss, he has many positive qualities. What makes him and the others weird is that their negative qualities both overshadow and dominate their Christian life and testimony.

Our approach must be, then, to learn what we can from our weird Christians and, at the same time, avoid the error of their ways.

What Ed Got Right

Probably the first thing Ed got right is that he has studied (many times) the book of Revelation. This is in sharp distinction to many of his "normal" brethren, who tend to avoid it. In this respect he has grasped the fact that 2 Timothy 3:16, *"All Scripture is God-breathed and is useful,"* includes the book of Revelation.

He does not avoid prophetic literature, but rather is attracted to it, both in the Old and New Testament. He also tries to see world events and news in the light of God's Word. He therefore understands the urgency of living in the last days and tends not to sink into apathy or lukewarmness.

He is, in the words of Theological Theo (who we will meet later), attempting to view himself eschatologically, and for this he is to be commended.

So What's Wrong with That?

The first problem that Ed faces is the other side of the aforementioned, and to be commended, study of the book of Revelation. It turns out that this is the only book he has ever studied! Ed survives on a sole diet of the theological version of future shock.

Motivated by fear, not faith

Ed, as a result, can be both negative and fatalistic. His perspective becomes muddy, and, rather than going out and preaching the Gospel from the starting point of God's love, he can tend to speak to others through, and motivate them by, fear of the future. He fails to emphasize faith in Jesus' sacrifice on the cross rather than fear of tribulation and judgment day.

Ed, you see, orders his behavior in the light of end-time prophecy rather than by the principles of God's Word. He may have purchased a seven-year supply of tribulation food supplies and a gun to protect them, not realizing that if Christians are destined to live through the tribulation (something that even End-Time Eds argue about), the commandment to love our neighbor, and for that matter our enemies, and God's promises of divine provision, are still the same.

Is It Really There?

Ed can also be guilty of eisegesis. That is, he is so keen to discover biblical meaning in today's political and social events that he can often read things into Scripture. He reminds me of the little old lady trying to commend her pastor for the excellent Sunday morning message he had just delivered. "Dear Pastor," she commented, "Thank you so much for your preaching. You seem to get so much out of the Bible that isn't really there!"

A few words in the book of Ezekiel or an obscure verb tense in an unusual Greek word can cause him to declare dogmatically the identity of the Antichrist or the number of vultures circling the valley of Megiddo.

The average Christian views this kind of thing as gentle and harmless banter, a sort of eschatological Trivial Pursuit. Not Ed, he takes it all very seriously and sometimes appears to be on a crusade of such intensity that one wonders how effective he would be if he could turn his passion to such things as evangelism, worship, or service.

Ed also enjoys fixing dates for the rapture and the millennium, but is always careful to tell you afterward that one must not do this. His case, of course, being an exception: "I am not saying that the Bible is clearly saying this, BUT..."

I remember hearing one prophecy teacher declare quite convincingly in late 1979 that he had spent over forty years studying the book of Revelation and felt there was no one else in the Western world as knowledgeable as himself on its subject matter. He then added that he didn't see how the rapture of the church and the second advent of Christ could happen any later than 1987.

"Now, I personally don't believe that one should set dates, BUT...I really think Christ will come again in the year 2769. How do I know this? Well, it's a complicated theory based on the numbering system from ancient Hebrew. I won't bore you with the details."

But the most important thing about this date is that it is well after the "prophet's" lifetime. This is a very important principle! I personally cannot understand why the majority of End-Time Eds have not caught on to this yet. I mean "89 reasons for 2089" has a much safer ring to it than "10 reasons for 2010" ever did! To set a date just a few years hence is to risk all future credibility and reputation for the sake of a few extra book or tape sales today!

End-
Time
Ed

Looking over His Shoulder

Ed can also be a little bit paranoid. He used to be very wary of credit cards, especially when they first came out. This was clearly the beginning of a worldwide economic system that would be controlled by the Antichrist. However, now that credit card use is so pandemic, Ed now draws the line on having more than a couple of credit cards. The worst credit card to have in one's possession is the Bankcard, which is available in some parts of the world. Not only does Bankcard start with the letter "B," the same first letter as the Beast, but one can also clearly see three sixes in the different outlines of the small "b" on the card itself. Coincidence? I think not!

Quick to believe any theory, doctrine, or insight

Interest over the number 666 is something that is understood by most Christians. The Bible clearly states that this number will in some way reveal the identity of the Antichrist (Revelation 13:18). Yet, our friend's paranoia can reach epic proportions. Eds have been known to refuse license plates and the purchase of clothes and real estate if this number is in any way part of the registration, address, or price tag. He fails to recognize that 666 is a very nice number. It is after 665 and before

667 and only has significance as a numerical value of the Antichrist's name during the tribulation.

I Believe!

One other problem Ed tends to have is something we are all susceptible to: He is very quick to believe any theory, doctrine, or insight into Scripture if it looks like it backs up his own particular views. He would declare to you quite boldly that vultures are laying eight times as many eggs in the Megiddo area in preparation for Armageddon. Not because he has researched the matter, but simply because it reinforces his belief system.

Tragically then, Ed spends so much of his time and energy consumed with prophecy and end times that he rarely has time for anything else. Issues such as personal character, holiness, serving the local church, evangelism, giving, and the like are ignored. "The End" is worshipped more than He who is both the beginning and the end. This fact, and this fact alone, is what, in the final analysis, classifies Ed as one of our weird Christians.

END-TIME ED

- Favorite Scripture: Revelation 6:12–17

- Least Favorite Scripture: Genesis through Jude

- Favorite TV Program: News

- Gets along well with Gullible Garfield and Demonic Dave

- Dislikes Frank Faith, who is too positive

- Catchphrase: "Beware the Mark"

3

PENTECOSTAL PAMELA

the holy spirit told me i'm right

Most of us have run into a Pentecostal Pamela at least one time in our lives. If nothing else, we have at least seen her from the pew as she grabs the microphone yet one more time to share a prophecy or Scripture verse. Pam is ever-eager to share what God has been doing in her life, something we can all learn from. But, while her intentions may appear sincere, she is also anxious to compare her spiritual walk with yours—a much less admirable quality.

Pam can usually be found at church, since she is there just about 24–7. If she is not in a prayer meeting or a Bible study, she is often in the pastor's office having a spiritual break-through.

Good for You, Pam

Pamela has many positive qualities. Indeed, a large proportion of the church world would do well to catch some of her fervor and obvious love for God. Her commitment to Christ is unquestioned. She is usually one of the most faithful attenders at the local church. In fact, she will be there at every service and participate in every small group (whether her husband likes it or not).

The reason Pamela is so excited is that she has learned—and, more importantly, experienced—the power of the Holy Spirit in her life. She is obedient to the Scripture in 1 Corinthians 14:1 that declares: *"Desire spiritual gifts."*

She is also one of the first in the church to see the value and power of prayer. As a result, she has kept many a prayer meeting from dying and inspired many of her fellow believers to develop a closer walk with Christ.

Danger Territory

The first disturbing attribute Pamela tends to develop is an attitude—an attitude that makes you feel that if you haven't experienced God like she has, then you are a sort of second-class Christian. This elitism is not limited to individuals; it can spread to whole churches and denominations. Pamela does not recognize the unity and diversity in the body of Christ and, consequently, if other believers do not think, act, talk, or dress exactly like her, then they are obviously missing it.

There seem to be no grays in Pamela's life— just black and white, right and wrong, my way or the highway. The truth that other churches and believers, who love God as passionately as she does, can experience Him in different ways is totally incomprehensible to her.

When this attitude takes hold of an entire church, it can lead to isolationism, where people begin to withdraw from everyone who might challenge them or speak into their lives. Such withdrawal is often total: withdrawal from those of different persuasions within the Christian church; withdrawal from those who

Pentecostal
Pamela

don't know Christ (because Pamelas fear contamination); withdrawal from friends and relatives; withdrawal from being part of this world coupled with a refusal to keep up-to-date with what is happening in the community, the country, indeed the whole of civilization. They choose to simply read the Bible and pray.

Although this sounds very noble, it quickly produces a fortress mentality within the believer. Everything is "us and them." Whatever is outside the group is seen as evil, and whatever is within is right.

Whatever is outside the group is seen as evil and whatever is within is right

---

This type of direction within the life of a Christian or a church is incredibly damaging in many different ways. It will certainly slow Pamela down, if not put a complete stop to her evangelistic effectiveness, as she loses both contact and understanding with the very people she is called to reach.

I firmly believe that, in order to be responsible Christians in this day and age, we need to keep in touch with our culture so we can minister effectively within it. Jesus was up-to-date with current events. He understood the problems people were grappling with and spoke God's Word into these situations. Culture is a moving target, and the call to be contemporary is not about being trendy; rather, it is a realization that the mission of the church must be our driving force and our chief consideration.

Best in Show

Another source of confusion in Pamela's life can be the area of internal versus external spirituality. Pamela can often confuse true godliness with external show. Dress, makeup, head coverings, lack of TVs, etc., are seen as more important than internal qualities such as humility, love, and patience. Worldliness, in Pamela's mind, is living as the world lives. This is measured by fashion labels, jargon, following sports, and the like. When the Bible speaks of worldliness, however, it speaks of carnality, strife, pride, and living for oneself rather than for God and others. First Corinthians 3:3 puts it this way: *"You are still worldly. For since there is jealousy and quarreling among you, are you not worldly? Are you not acting like mere men?"*

The church I grew up in viewed spirituality in this narrow and superficial way. I remember being taught that it was wrong to go to the movies, not based on the content of the film, but based on the teachings of Psalm 1. I wasn't to know that David probably didn't have moviegoing in mind when he penned these words: *"Blessed is the man who does not walk in the counsel of the wicked or stand in the way of sinners or sit in the seat of mockers"* (verse 1). When one enters

Pentecostal Pamela

35

a movie theater and sits down, he may unknowingly be sitting in a seat that was previously occupied by a mocker of God, thus clearly doing exactly the opposite of David's imperative.

Puts church above family

I gradually realized that, if taken to its logical conclusion, such thinking would prohibit all sitting down anywhere: park benches, grassy slopes, secondhand cars. Slowly the condemnation lifted, and I binged on eight films in a week. I felt I was free to enjoy James Bond and *Saturday Night Fever*. (Did I use the word *enjoy*?!) In this video age, such false reasoning seems ridiculous. I believe we should guard what we watch and what we listen to, but it is the content, and not the genre, we should be critical of. For most of us, it is what we watch, not the act of watching, that can lead us astray.

Confused Priorities

Pamela also has a tendency to put the church above her family. This can bring incredible stress into her marriage. Her husband, if a Christian, is never as spiritual as she is because he tends to be more down-to-earth, practical, and not as intense (a little bit like Paul, Mary, Esther, James, John, Ruth, and Jesus).

She often prays for her husband, sometimes in public in a super-spiritual, patronizing way, which, if he is not a Christian, will certainly guarantee he never takes that step.

While we are speaking of marriage, we probably need to bring up the subject of sex, something that Pamela will never do because sex to her is, more often than not, either: a) sinful; b) a necessary evil; c) an unnecessary evil; d) okay, but not as good as praying together!

In summary, Pamela is intense and emotional. She dislikes those who "think" a lot about the Bible or God. She is constantly praying or prophesying (in King James English) for those who don't quite see things as she does.

Pentecostal
Pamela

PENTECOSTAL PAMELA

- Favorite Scripture: Acts, Colossians 3:2, and the clothing and food laws in Leviticus, Numbers, and Deuteronomy

- Least Favorite Scriptures: Romans and Galatians

- Favorite TV Program: Doesn't have a TV

- Gets along well with Gullible Garfield and Demonic Dave

- Dislikes Backslidden Bob and Theological Theo

- Catchphrase: "You are not free until you dance in church"

THEOLOGICAL
THEO

dying by degrees

Many of us at some time or another have encountered a Theological Theo. They are reasonably simple to spot within the Christian church and will nearly always give themselves away when they open their mouths. They often mutter to themselves in Greek, Hebrew, or Aramaic, and words like *synoptic* and *kenosis* flow from their lips. They are more serious than the average Christian. Their Bibles are larger and heavier, cross-referenced, and color-coded, with what appears to be unreadable scribble jotted in the margins.

Many of today's Theos, however, have traded these unwieldy forms of identification for the latest model laptop, which they open with relish at local Bible study groups, much to the intimidation of the other participants.

When Theo speaks, we normally listen, because Theo knows what he is talking about and seems to have answers to every question.

What can we learn from Theo's life?

Theo, on the Right Track

We can and must learn from what Theo does: Primarily, he studies God's Word constantly and thoroughly. He treats the Bible with the reverence it deserves. He wants to get at the truth and understand the plain meaning of the text. He refuses to treat the Bible as a collection of quotations—the wit and wisdom of God—or, even worse, as some kind of subjective document where each person's interpretation is as valid as the next. No, Theo is keen on rightly dividing God's Word.

Studies God's Word constantly and thoroughly

One of his pet peeves is the tendency many Christians have of playing fast and loose with the Bible, picking verses, or even parts of verses, out of context.

He is quick to point out that many men and women have labored hard and long in the area of paleography, studying the earliest manuscripts in Greek Coptic, Syriac, and Phoenician. They have done this so that today's Greek text, upon which modern translations are based, draws its accuracy from well over twenty thousand different papyrus fragments, manuscripts, and codexes. Many scholars have devoted their lives so that we might have confidence in the accuracy of God's Word. Even the punctuation marks are the subject of much technical debate and should not be unthinkingly swept aside just so we can make the Bible say what we want it to say. This esteem for God's Word is something we should all seek to adopt.

Such an approach to Scripture has many benefits. Chief among them is that Theo will rarely be deceived, as he carefully checks things out, comparing Scripture with Scripture. He does not just believe whatever he hears or reads. The greatest preacher in the church world today or the author of best-selling books doesn't impress Theo. He simply cross-references, checks things out, and examines the context before he accepts what is being said.

Theo knows not only what he believes, but why he believes it. He is able to give an answer and a defense for the hope that lies within him (1 Peter 3:15).

Off the Tracks

While there is a lot we can learn from Theo, there is much to be wary of as well.

Theo can often be afflicted with a sort of religious, intellectual pride that was exemplified by the Pharisees and Sadducees of Jesus' day. This can often cause him, as it did them, to miss the truth when they are face-to-face with it, easily dismissing other Christians' opinions, especially if they don't have scholarly degrees.

We have already seen that devotion to study is admirable, yet study is merely step one in a two-step process. We are to study in order to do. Learning is a prerequisite to action. Unfortunately, many Theos get stuck in the accumulation of knowledge phase, never moving on to the application of the knowledge, which is, of course, what Christianity is all about.

James 1:22–25 brings this to the forefront:

Do not merely listen to the word, and so deceive yourselves. Do what it says. Anyone who listens to the word but does not do what it says is like a man who looks at his face in a mirror and, after looking at himself, goes away and immediately forgets what he looks like. But the man who looks intently into the perfect law that gives freedom, and continues to do this, not forgetting what he has heard, but doing it—he will be blessed in what he does.

One of the values of our church in Perth, and a truth we continually try to champion, is that church is about helping people live the Christian life in an authentic and practical way. Truth must be translated into action. The Christian life is not just about what we believe but about how we live. Church services, therefore, should be education, not entertainment; education with take-home, real-life value.

The blessing, joy, and fulfillment of the Christian life is in its living. There is nothing wrong with inspecting the ingredients and studying the menu, but the proof of the pudding is in the eating.

I'm Not Feeling It

Another blind spot Theo can develop has to do with the power of emotion. Pascal had insight into this when he penned the phrase, "Pious scholars rare." He meant that if one develops only one area of life, the other departments tend to suffer. The athlete is rarely a scholar as well. The scholar, one who has spent much time and energy in the development of the intellectual world, can often be a dwarf in the world of emotions or spirituality.

Removes the emotional from his Christian experience

The scholar, because his focus has been on developing the intellectual world, can often be anti-emotional. He dislikes strong passion or being with people who show their feelings. Church services where people are excited, jump around, or, worse still, raise their hands are to be avoided. Theo simply labels such outbursts as superficial.

In this he fails to understand that God has created us as emotional beings and that much Scripture, particularly Psalms, has to do with allowing our heartfelt, as well as head-reasoned, faith to expose itself. The medicine of laughter, the release of tears, the show of physical affection are all part of what being human is all about. To remove these from our experience is to become incomplete.

Many Theos not only have a bias against emotion but also against the supernatural.

When the intellect reigns, the miraculous begins to find itself edged out. Theos can quickly begin to demythologize Scripture. That is, they remove anything that doesn't seem to make sense to the natural mind in an attempt to make God more palatable to our rational Western society.

Theo finds it easier to believe that the Red Sea didn't really part: "The water was just very shallow." The resurrection is reduced to metaphor: "It is the spirit of the teachings of Christ that continue to live on." Such statements make a lot of sense to Theo, yet the difficulties of drowning Pharaoh's army in knee-deep water and explaining how Christianity became the fastest growing religious movement in the ancient world without an empty tomb are questions that are not deeply considered.

One of Theo's worst faults is his delight in theological language. He will discuss at length the difference between kerygma and didache, the application of the Granville Sharp Rule in Ephesians 4, and the Messianic Secret without bothering to explain what is meant by these terms. Consequently, only the initiated can follow any of his new theological revelations. Unfortunately, very few theologians write for the layperson, and as a result, the fruit of their labors are only enjoyed by other scholars. This is one of the reasons why Theo is not as popular as he thinks he should be within Christian circles. The jargon, the hint of intellectual pride, and the desire to explain away the supernatural are all things that rub Pentecostal Pamela the wrong way.

Theological Theo

So, Pentecostal Pamela, and a good many other Christians, tend to throw the baby out with the bathwater, dismissing all Theological Theos. The aversion to biblical study that is common in many churches often has a liberal, pedantic, and abstruse Theo at its roots.

In summary, I believe Theo's main problem is not his emphasis on study, but the fact that he emphasizes it too much. Other elements to the Christian life, such as faith and prayer, rarely get a second thought.

Loves jargon and has a hint of intellectual pride

I remember well the early days of our church here in Perth. A local Theological Theo came to one of our services. He had been in Christian ministry for about ten years and held several doctorates in various areas of Christian theology and philosophy. Our church had been in existence for five years or so and numbered somewhere between six hundred and seven hundred people. My father, with one year of Bible training under his belt, was the pastor.

The service was pretty standard. Several people came to Christ, and a sense of God's presence, both in corporate worship and in the teaching and prayer, was clearly evident. Theo's reaction was one of intense anger. Theo was mad (which, emotionally speaking, was a very positive step forward for him). He was mad because he had devoted nearly a decade to study and preparation, and now, after ten years of active ministry, he had seen only a few people's lives touched in a real way. Yet here were others who had neither the knowledge nor skill at handling the text, and yet it seemed that God was blessing them. He failed to understand that prayer and faith, as well as study, are prerequisites for successful ministry.

Theo sometimes fails to realize that lives will not change without the movement of the Spirit of God upon His Word and His people. Let me be quick to add that when Theo realizes this and begins to prioritize his life correctly, he will rapidly turn out to be one of the greatest assets to the local church. His teachings will become one of the keys to sustained revival.

Theological
Theo

THEOLOGICAL THEO

- Favorite Scriptures: 2 Timothy 3:15, John 1:1 (in the original Greek)

- Least Favorite Scriptures: Acts, 1 Corinthians 14

- Favorite TV Programs: Documentaries

- Gets along well with other Theological Theos

- Dislikes Gullible Garfield

- Catchphrase: Doesn't believe in simplistic clichés

DEMONIC DAVE

the devil made me do it

Demonic Dave is another colorful character found among Christians around the globe. Although his natural habitat tends to be within Pentecostal or charismatic churches, sightings have been reported in all denominations of the Christian church.

The Lessons We Can Learn

Dave has many things to teach us, and like all weird Christians, the truth that he has embraced in his life is one that many fellow believers have failed to come to grips with at all. Dave understands both the reality and the danger of the Devil and demonic forces.

He has not made the mistake of relegating these things to ancient days, as have many of his contemporaries, who see demonic forces as a sort of quaint anachronism in our modern culture. Neither has he succumbed to the belief that if demonic activity is real then it only takes place in Third World countries. Dave in these areas is, of course, quite correct. Jesus spent a whole lot of time and energy teaching us that we do have an enemy. Jesus' ministry was not characterized simply by teaching, preaching, and healings but by exorcisms as well.

The apostle Paul picked this theme up, especially in Ephesians 6, and tried to make the Christian aware that the dimension we are battling in is not a physical one but a spiritual one. Our enemy is not only our flesh and the culture we find ourselves in; there is a very real supernatural army arrayed against us as well.

> *Put on the full armor of God so that you can take your stand against the devil's schemes. For our struggle is not against flesh and blood, but against the rulers, against the authorities, against the powers of this dark world and against the spiritual forces of evil in the heavenly realms.* (Ephesians 6:11–12)

Dave has received much encouragement in recent years, as many churches have grabbed these truths through widespread teaching on subjects like intercession and spiritual warfare. Dave will often be seen in the front rows of such seminars with a smug expression on his face as if to say, "Finally, people are waking up to this vital aspect of Christian faith and experience."

Yet on the Other Hand...

The trouble is, of course, that for Dave this is not an aspect of the truth but the whole truth. This now familiar deception of overemphasis is clearly seen in the life of Demonic Dave.

Dave not only knows more about the Devil and demonic forces than he does about God, but he has, in many cases, a greater respect for them. He has more faith in Satan's ability to destroy and thwart the plans of God than

Demonic
Dave

the other way around. It is not because he doesn't believe in God or because he doesn't view the Devil as the enemy; it is just that he has spent so much time studying, thinking on, and warning others about satanic strategy and influence that he has lost overall perspective. It's a little bit like being so overawed by the power of a small arsenal of automatic and semiautomatic rifles that you forget you have a few thousand Stealth Fighters on your side.

He is more conscious of the Devil's presence than he is of God's

Dave is certainly more conscious of the Devil's presence than he is of God's, and he tends to be able to discern and hear the enemy's voice clearer and with more frequency than he does his heavenly Father's.

Dave's favorite meetings are, of course, when an evangelist who specializes in this type of ministry hits town. People are invited to the front who have any type of problem. They are then immediately diagnosed en masse as being demonically oppressed or possessed. Subsequent delivery sessions, complete with screaming, seizures, and even vomiting, all add to the occasion and form the list of vital ingredients for what Dave would call a "great meeting."

The reason Dave loves this type of meeting is that deep down Dave believes that nearly all the problems we face are in some way demon-related. Many stories have been told of famous Demonic Daves in history who have cast out spirits of selfishness, pride, education, lust, and chocolate. You name it, and he has probably cast it out!

We must be cautious not to jump to the other extreme, where we exclude demonic oppression or possession as the cause of, or the compounding of, any of the problems humanity faces. Yet the Bible speaks far more of the lusts of the flesh and the pressures of society than it does of specific demons. In my experience, ninety-nine times out of one hundred, people do not need demonic deliverance. What they need is to crucify the flesh, begin to nurture the fruits of the Spirit, and be transformed by the renewing of their minds. Though I must admit, it certainly would be an easier and simpler world if the ratio of demons to problems was a lot higher. If that were the case, we could simply be prayed for and have our problems expelled.

Freedom without decision from overeating, pride, or sexual promiscuity, has a wonderful allure. Yet terms such as discipline, faithfulness, persistence, and forgiveness have real meaning and do make a difference. We are not puppets controlled either by God or the Devil. We have a huge part to play ourselves. Control of our lives will not be taken by God, and cannot be taken by the enemy, without much effort and inclination on our part.

Demonic
Dave

Very Real, Very Defeated

Probably one of the great truths of the New Testament that Dave has failed to recognize is that Satan, who is very real, is also very defeated. Hebrews 2:14 declares: *"Since the children have flesh and blood, he too shared in their humanity so that by his death he might destroy him who holds the power of death—that is, the devil."*

Doesn't realize that what Christ has done is more powerful than what the Devil is doing

---

The Greek word for *"destroy"* here (as Theological Theo would point out) is the word *katargeo,* which means, "to render useless, to make of no effect" (*Strong's Exhaustive Concordance of the Bible* G#2673). This simply means that Satan's existence is taken for granted, but his power is relegated to intimidation, temptation, and persuasion. He is the accuser more than he is the attacker. He suggests and subverts, for he can do no other. The head-on, full-frontal attack is no longer an option since his bombers carry no bombs and his missile silos are empty.

The Devil can bluff and frequently does. He can accuse and scare, and he lies because he has to. Those who really have the power have no need to lie. Lying is the strategy of the desperate, and Satan's constant use of this tactic should cause all of us to realize the hopelessness of his position.

Demonic Dave must realize that what Christ has done and is doing is far more important and more powerful than what the Devil is doing. Even though we should be on our guard and not act with naiveté when it comes to the warfare we find ourselves in, we should also not give too much thought to our enemy.

I personally believe that the best form of attack is not to spend energy on interesting, yet unbiblical, strategies such as spiritual mapping, but instead to simply go about doing what Christ has commanded. We must obey our commission—preaching the Gospel, praying for the sick, helping the poor, and thereby growing the community of God.

Demonic
Dave

DEMONIC DAVE

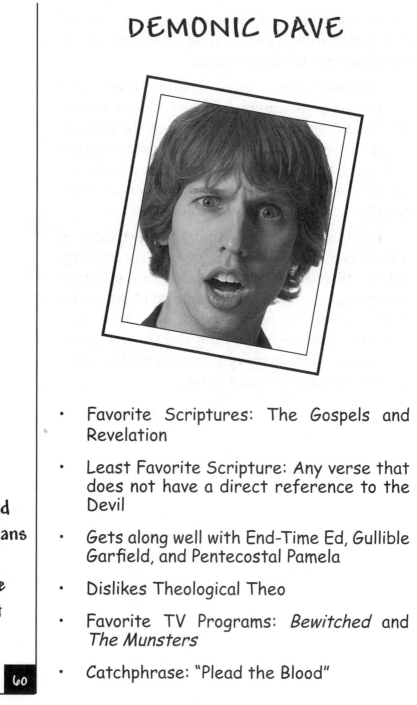

- Favorite Scriptures: The Gospels and Revelation

- Least Favorite Scripture: Any verse that does not have a direct reference to the Devil

- Gets along well with End-Time Ed, Gullible Garfield, and Pentecostal Pamela

- Dislikes Theological Theo

- Favorite TV Programs: *Bewitched* and *The Munsters*

- Catchphrase: "Plead the Blood"

6

FRANK
FAITH

i don't believe i'm weird

Frank Faith is a fairly recent phenomenon. It would be hard to find one who predates 1970. The reason Frank suddenly popped up all over the place is that the Christian world began to get a little morbid and fatalistic. "Nothing happens unless God allows it" and "Whatever will be will be" were catchphrases of the age. The church world, by and large, settled back to see what God was going to do within the next few years rather than taking Him at His word and believing that faith in God could, and would, make a difference.

So Frank, despite his failings, had a lot of good things to teach the church, as do all our weird Christians.

Don't Forget the Power of Faith

The power of faith is probably the greatest lesson Frank has taught and continues to teach. He is quick to point out that our faith in God can and will affect and influence our futures—that although God is God, He delights in and seeks out people when they begin to believe in Him. Frank, then, is always trying to encourage people to believe and is always ready to believe God himself. "Whatever the problem, whatever the situation you are facing, let's pray, let's believe, let's claim God's Word and see the results."

This attitude leads Frank to be pretty much an optimist because he sincerely believes that

God can and will respond and bring answers in every situation. He has a very positive attitude and usually raises the hopes of people around him, unlike, of course, End-Time Ed, who tends to deflate them. (Just a side note: When organizing a Christian party or barbecue, think carefully about the ratio of End-Time Eds to Frank Faiths. It is probably necessary to invite two Frank Faiths for every one End-Time Ed unless you want to see all the guests leave early!)

Word People

Another positive quality Frank brings to the table is his love and enthusiasm for God's Word. He understands that faith comes from hearing the Word of God (Romans 10:17) and therefore realizes that, in order to feed his faith, he needs lots of Bible intake. This is an admirable and essential quality. Frank pushes this so much that he and his friends refer to one another as "Word people" and to their churches as "Word churches," with the subtle implication that other churches and Christians don't really believe God's Word.

So why is all that weird? Well, of course, Frank would not be referred to as weird if what we have discussed so far is all there is to him. Frank, however, again falls prey to the trap of allowing one truth to become "the truth." The blinders this puts on his eyes and mind often lead him to go astray in many areas of his life.

Where Frank Goes Wrong

Probably the first way Frank can get off track is that he begins to apply his faith in every situation. Although we can marvel at his passion, we must be watchful of his methods. He is quick to believe God not only for the obvious but also for those things where hard work and simple obedience are more called for. Faith is almost seen as a convenient escape from such notions of diligence and discipline. This type of Christian applies his faith to losing weight while maintaining normal food intake and exercise levels (which were totally responsible for the excess weight in the first place!).

Has more passion in believing God for the mundane than in believing Him for what really matters

---

Frank, in fact, has more passion in believing God for the mundane and the banal than for the stuff that really matters: lifestyle more than lost people; car model more than character. Frank Faiths have been known to believe for a wink from someone else's wife or that God would get rid of the pastor they didn't particularly like even though he loves them, prays for them, and teaches them the Bible.

"Well, he's not a Word person, like I am." "God needs to send us someone more mature." This kind of harsh judgment and spiritual elitism is commonplace among Franks. The funny thing is, they don't even seem to realize it. Another's perceived lack of faith is seen as a far worse trait than the act of judging and condemning them for it.

Frank often chooses to criticize people because of their poor confessions. These can be anything from "I feel tired" to "I've got a bit of a cold" to "I'm not sure what I'm going to do." Yet he fails to realize that these very same people may very well be exercising a far deeper level of faith as they pray and believe God for their next door neighbor's salvation or for strength to overcome challenges in their internal world. Frank may be using his faith, for which he is to be commended, but those he often criticizes are actually living by theirs.

Faith in Faith

Probably the greatest danger Frank can slip into is when he begins to develop faith in faith. Faith itself becomes the main thing. In other words, it ceases to become the agent through which one receives and instead it becomes the main focus.

When a person receives salvation through faith, it is always understood that God is the One who does the saving work and that faith is merely the means by which we appropriate what Christ has already done for us.

One of my teachers on the book of Romans painted the picture of God giving us a burning hot coal, which is salvation. We find it impossible to pick it up without burning ourselves. So God then places in our hands some tongs, and by means of the tongs, we are able to take hold of the salvation that God has given. Now tongs are good and useful, and it is wonderful that they are supplied in this manner, but they are merely a means to an end.

Frank Faith gets this confused. He mistakes the tongs for God and is constantly buying tapes and books with titles like *Seven Steps to Increasing the Size of Your Tongs*. He is always attending seminars on how to use tongs more effectively. On visiting his home, you are shown with much pride the tongs collection hanging on the wall. God, the giver of both the tongs and the coal, the faith and the salvation, is left out of the loop. This is the fallacy of faith in faith. God becomes superfluous, and the means through which we receive becomes the very goal and center of victorious Christian living. When faith takes on this kind of dynamic, it becomes something we can be proud of! I mean, after all, "It is because of my great faith that God has done all these things for me!"

If this is true, faith has become a work—the noblest of all works, yet still a work. Those who work it will receive, those who don't, won't. In this way, salvation is limited to those who do the faith-job correctly. Clearly the whole intent of the New Testament is that faith is not a work in this sense; it is simply an open heart trusting God with sincerity and passion.

Frank makes faith a work—a noble work, but still a work

Faith is a little like a man thrown from the boat in the midst of a storm. He reaches out his hands and cries, "Help me! Save me!" and in response, the life buoy is thrown—not as a reward for a good work but from a motive of love, with both the ability and the willingness to save. The outstretched hands were merely the means through which the offered salvation was received.

Faith Front

Finally, I personally feel that the greatest fault, and consequently the greatest harm, that Frank Faith has and can do is in the area of personal transparency in living as an authentic Christian.

Over the years I have observed many Frank Faiths. I admit that for a few years I even was one myself! The answer to every problem is to confess and believe, and not to do this is to be condemned and judged. So, regardless of the problems one may be facing in life—grief, marriage difficulties, threat of disease, depression—one could never really be honest. The "faith front" was what was required. This can result in whole churches being filled with plastic Christians, saying the right things, believing the right things, but inwardly diminishing. The Bible, you see, also teaches that we are to *"bear one another's burdens"* (Galatians 6:2 NKJV), to *"rejoice with those who rejoice, and weep with those who weep"* (Romans 12:15 NKJV). We must share honestly with one another the mountains we face, and then together believe that God will walk with us and deliver us.

Faith should never ignore the problem. Indeed, faith admits to it and then looks for solutions from the God dimension rather than simply human endeavor. Honest, transparent, struggling Christians have, in my experience, been far more effective in evangelism, far more emotionally healthy, and far more likely to be in the race for the long term. Frank Faiths, by and large, burn out quick or become bitter over time. Let us learn the lessons that Frank teaches us! Let us believe God together and feed upon His Word, keeping God and our growth in Him preeminent in our thinking and lives!

FRANK FAITH

- Favorite Scriptures: Mark 11:24 and Philippians 4:13

- Least Favorite Scriptures: 1 Peter, Job, and the Prophets

- Gets along well with Gullible Garfield

- Dislikes End-Time Ed (because he's too negative)

- Favorite TV Program: *Ripley's Believe It or Not!*

- Catchphrase: "That's a bad confession"

7

BACKSLIDDEN BOB

slip sliding away

Backslidden Bob is almost in a category of his own when it comes to weird Christians. He is weird in a different way than many of the others. His weirdness is not because of an overemphasis on a certain truth or value. No, he is weird in the sense that he is not doing, or even attempting to do, what he was designed to do.

Not doing what he was designed to do

Romans 12:1 sheds some light on this:

I beseech you therefore, brethren, by the mercies of God, that you present your bodies a living sacrifice, holy, acceptable to God, which is your reasonable service. (NKJV)

Theo would point out that the word *"reasonable"* here is the Greek word *logikos,* from which we get our English words *logic* and *logical.* Paul was saying that, to be logical as a Christian, one is to live a fully devoted life. A halfhearted approach to Christianity is nonsense in that it is living contrary to what we were designed for.

When I lived at Bondi Beach in Sydney, I was always dismayed by a little old lady who used to drive her brand-new Ferrari over the hill from Double Bay to go for her morning walk along the beach. The Ferrari had never been over 30 mph, and as I used to walk by it each day, I could hear its voice calling me. "Help me! Save me! Drive me!" I know, you know, and the Ferrari knew that that kind of car is designed to be driven—I mean *really* driven. And for it to putter along at 30 mph was a travesty of design and a crime of huge proportion! It simply didn't make sense. It is logical for a bird to fly because that is what it is designed for. It is logical for a yacht to be sailed and a television to be watched. The plane that spends its entire life in a museum, like the "Spruce Goose" tourist attraction in McMinnville, Oregon, is in this sense, weird.

Backslidden Bob is this kind of weird Christian. He is failing to be who he is and lives life, in the words of poet Ezra Pound, as one filled with "barren regret."

So Has Bob Got Anything Good to Say?

Surprisingly, Bob does have something to teach us. But here we must not look at what Bob does or doesn't do, but rather at the motives behind his choice of Christian lifestyle. You see, Bob doesn't like super-spiritual Christians and, more often than not, has been turned off to authentic Christianity by hanging around or being married to some variety of plastic believer. It could have been a Pentecostal Pamela or a Frank Faith or variations on these characters—whoever it was, he or she had an effect. Deep down, Bob thinks to himself, "If that is what serving Christ is all about, then I can't compete. I must not have the necessary raw material from which to build a life as a devoted follower of Christ." In so reasoning, Bob throws out the baby with the bathwater and is guilty of believing that the false image portrayed by the Christians he is in contact with is the biblical image of what serving God is all about.

Bob is probably one of those guys who is quick to put himself down on spiritual matters but actually has a discernment and sense of right and wrong that goes far beyond the typical weird Christian. He sees things like religious tradition and the unthinking acceptance of all teaching. He tends not to take himself too seriously and is therefore quick to laugh at himself, his mistakes, and the mistakes of the church. This often gets him into a lot of trouble because his position is often seen to be rebellious.

We must relate to our world and influence others for Christ

He also has a strong sense of mission in that he firmly believes we must relate to our world and influence others for Christ. He has realized, unlike many, that the religious model repels rather than attracts the non-Christian. So, in an attempt to say, "You can be a Christian and still be normal," he moves closer and closer to the values and behavior of his unsaved friends until the difference is essentially imperceptible. He calls this identification, empathy, and evangelism.

Unfortunately, from the rest of the church's perception and from a biblical perspective, he has compromised from being "in the world but not of the world," to being very much a part of it. His salt is in contact with lost humanity, but its impact is negligible for it has lost its potency.

D. L. Moody said, "The place for the ship is in the sea, but God help the ship if the sea gets into it." This is what has happened to Bob. His testimony, values, and finally, beliefs drown in the ocean that surrounds him.

No Evidence to Convict

Bob definitely fits the bill of the invisible Christian. The old saying, "If it was against the law to be a Christian, would there be enough evidence to convict you?" finds its real fulfillment with the Bobs among us.

To be sure, Bob is not super-spiritual. The trouble is, he is not even slightly spiritual. This attempt to keep his light from shining causes internal disorientation and renders his potential to influence other people for God null and void. When an opportunity comes up to share what he really believes to a friend or relative, his words have no real weight apart from shock value. The response often goes along these lines: "What! You're a Christian? You've got to be kidding! I never knew that about you." This response may be considered normal in a casual friendship, but when it's your parent or lifelong buddy, then it's another matter.

Stuck in a Rut

Bob is in the ditch on one side of the Christian road while in the ditch on the other side are most of the other weird Christians we have looked at thus far. Bob may be in a different ditch, but he is still not moving forward and progressing in his journey of Christian faith. His overreaction to legalistic or inauthentic Christianity is as bad a testimony as those he is trying to distance himself from.

The one thing that seems to turn a Bob around is a real encounter with authentic faith. If he can move beyond his cynicism for just a little while and encounter a good, biblically based, and balanced local community of believers, or a friend or colleague who shows sincere faith and love, then Bob can undergo an internal revolution. His hunger for truth will return. And yet, after so many encounters with imitation or abusive faith, he has almost thrown in the towel. His heart has been captured by a slow-growing, hardening skin of cynicism and doubt.

If he comes into contact with genuine Christianity, then the fire of his early days as a new Christian will gradually return. Basically, Bob needs to be challenged to be part of the answer rather than being part of the problem.

We can respond to hypocrisy in the church by joining it and walking away from our faith. Alternatively, we can choose to commit ourselves to following Christ, who opposed the religious oppression of His day and lived out what He believed, regardless of the prevailing peer pressure.

Courageous Bobs can and should be the pillars of our churches. Their discernment and down-to-earth approach are needed. Their cynicism and desertion are not.

Backslidden
Bob

BACKSLIDDEN BOB

- Favorite Scriptures: Song of Solomon and the Gospels

- Least Favorite Scriptures: The Epistles and the Pentateuch

- Favorite TV Program: Anything except televangelists

- Dislikes any other weird Christian but especially hates Pentecostal Pamela, End-Time Ed, and Demonic Dave

- Catchphrase: "I'm not weird"

GULLIBLE
GARFIELD

you're never going to believe this, but...

Gullible Garfield is a nice guy. Everyone says so. He is probably the most popular of all the weird Christians that we have looked at so far—this is especially true when he is among other weird Christians. His popularity is due to the fact that he is so agreeable. Pastors and teachers are another group that values him highly. There is nothing like having a few Gullible Garfields scattered among the congregation when teaching on a difficult subject. His encouraging nods and hearty "Amens" will give confidence to the most doubtful of theologies.

Garfield is not only the most popular; he is also the most commonly found. There are many varieties of Garfields, and most churches have a fair handful of them. So let's have a closer look at what makes a Gullible Garfield tick— what he brings to the Christian table and what he takes away from it as well.

We Can All Learn from That

Probably the primary positive quality that Gullible Garfield has is that he is so quick to believe in people. He is ready to trust and believes the best in every person he encounters. He has no problem with the messages of love, acceptance, and forgiveness and simply cannot understand how people like Theological Theo and Judgmental Jill can be so down on so many other Christians.

This attitude means that he is not only well liked but also able to encourage and motivate those around him. We all need acceptance and unconditional love, and Garfield is wired in a way that makes him able to give it.

Yet, on the Other Hand

The trouble with Garfield is that this uncritical acceptance is not just limited to people but includes beliefs, teachings, and Christian fads. He is willing to accept almost anybody, and for this he is to be commended. But he is also willing to accept almost any doctrine, and for this he must be cautioned.

I personally believe Garfield is responsible for the huge increase in the Christian book market over the last decade. It doesn't matter what sort of crazy teaching is published, there are at least one hundred thousand Garfields in the Western world ready to buy the latest volume all about it. This popularity, of course, only encourages him: "This must be true, the sales prove it!" Success, however, whether it is measured in book sales, ratings, figures, or church congregation size, is no indication of truth. If it were, both the Mormons and the Muslims are right, and Jesus, with His pitiful showing of only a handful of followers at His death, needs to be discarded.

Garfield, however, does not think these things through. He merely accepts. His opinion on any subject is usually the opinion of the person he last spoke to. Second Peter 2:1–3

Gullible
Garfield

tells us that we need to be careful what we hear; that among the good there is also the evil and that among the true prophets there are the false ones as well. Indeed, among the churches mentioned in Revelation 1–3, most had been affected by the scourge of false teachers. Even in the greatest sermon in history, the Sermon on the Mount, Jesus spent much time on the need to be discerning. *"Watch out for false prophets. They come to you in sheep's clothing, but inwardly they are ferocious wolves. By their fruit you will recognize them"* (Matthew 7:15–16).

His opinion is usually that of the person he last spoke to

The lack of biblical sensibility has led Garfield to lead an interesting and colorful life theologically. He quickly moves through different phases to the point that you could be mistaken in thinking you were meeting an entirely different person every time you ran into him. One month he is obsessed with spiritual warfare, the next prosperity. A year down the road he will be telling you the latest theories concerning the alignment of the planets, the end of the millennium, and the return of Christ. A few weeks later he has moved totally, both theologically and geographically, and will be living in some apartment in Toronto or Pensacola. There seems to be no stability, no underlying truths, no foundation upon which he is building. He is merely haphazardly flip-flopping through the varied kaleidoscope of Christian and fringe-Christian life, beliefs, and activity.

The following is a list of some of the things that your local Garfield may have believed and strongly promoted over the last few years:

1. Proctor and Gamble

This large, multinational corporation, makers of Bounty, Cover Girl, and many other household products, is apparently owned by the Church of Satan. A good portion of the money it makes goes to this cause. Garfield will have told you that the CEO of Proctor and Gamble appeared on *Donahue* and admitted this. As a result, the printing presses were fired up and the petitions went out worldwide to the church, imploring Christians not to buy any products from this demonically inspired company. Garfields around the country continue to believe this. Even now, long after the initial outcry began, petitions occasionally come across my desk.

The truth is, the whole thing is a lie. No one appeared on *Donahue*. The company is not owned by the Church of Satan and certainly does not give its money to any such organization. The Theological Theos who have researched this (one of their positive attributes) believe the whole thing was started up by a competing company. And what a successful strategy it has been! It has cost Proctor and Gamble millions of dollars in lost sales.

2. Discovery of Hell

Several years back it was reported in several European papers that a Russian mining experiment had left the miners and scientists associated with the project trembling in their boots. They had stumbled across what could only be described as "hell." Deep below the core of the earth, they broke into some kind of chasm, out of which came incredible heat and steam. When microphones were lowered down on massive cables, the sound of human screaming could be heard. The mine work quickly came to an end, the shafts were filled up, and the story was suppressed by the Western media.

Again, those who tried to nail this particular story came up empty every time. There is also the problem with the logistics of lowering microphones down miles of underground tunneling, as well as finding ones that would not melt when subjected to the incredible temperatures described.

Slowly, even the Garfields began to have their doubts, and the story died a slow death. Yet, who knows, it may have simply gone underground!

3. Jesus in the Clouds

Garfield probably carries one of these photos in his wallet. One can clearly see a cloud-like formation of Jesus standing in the sky with his arms outstretched. The picture was supposedly taken from the window of an airplane encountering severe turbulence. One of the passengers who was a strong believer began to pray and then felt led to take a photograph through the window. When the photo was developed, she was amazed to see the figure of Jesus.

Sadly, this person has never been found. The flight has been widely reported by Garfields around the world, however, each time the facts are slightly different. In one telling, it was a man on an Air India flight. In another, it was a young girl flying British Airways. The photo is always the same, yet the story varies and the real people vanish the moment anybody starts to check it out.

4. The Illuminati

I clearly remember this one from when I was in Bible college in 1979. A friend of mine sent me a tape of a man who had just come to Christ out of witchcraft. He was speaking about an amazing conspiracy between various branches of economic, political, and spiritual organizations with plans to take over the world

Gullible
Garfield

and usher in the reign of the Antichrist. This clandestine organization, headed by a ruling group called the Illuminati, was on schedule, and everything happening in world events was part of a carefully contrived plan. The truth was only being revealed now as a result of this man's conversion to Christianity.

The story spread like wildfire around the globe. (The tape I received had already been around the world once before I got it.) However, once again, study, research, and common sense showed the whole thing to be a sham.

Jumps to conclusions over minor coincidences

The whole conspiracy theory concept is one that is both perennial and popular with Gullible Garfields. Mystery syndicates and secretly aligned groups hold an unexplained fascination for the average Gullible Garfield. Why, even our own congregation was aligned to the New Age movement for a few months because part of our logo back then was a rainbow, which was one of the symbols of the New Age movement. It is amazing to me that people can jump to such conclusions over such minor coincidences. I thought the rainbow was a sign of God's promise—but what do I know?

I also think, after working with many different people and organizations, that to get more than two or three entities working together on a common project, while keeping it a secret, is next to impossible. Political, bureaucratic, and religious organizations are full of leaks. Even within the life of the local church, the moment two or three people know about a certain development, it seems everyone knows. Just imagine a group that could develop a comprehensive, organizational network that would have the power and potential to take over the world in every area and keep the whole thing a secret. Imagine if they could keep Ted Turner, *60 Minutes*, and the BBC all in the dark; ensure Murdoch and Fleet Street remained ignorant; and develop the computer and relational networks necessary to pull it all off. Any group or conspiracy able to do this probably deserves the world! It is the sort of thing, I think, that only God could do.

Gullible
Garfield

GULLIBLE GARFIELD

- Favorite Scripture: Whatever he's reading at the time.

- Least Favorite Scriptures: Jude and 2 Peter 2

- Favorite TV Programs: Commercials and professional wrestling

- Gets along well with everyone

- Catchphrase: "Amen"

9

JUDGMENTAL JILL

there's something in your eye

M ost of the weird Christians we have looked at so far have had some redeeming qualities. But I have been hard-pressed to think of some good things to say about the subject of this particular chapter.

I guess one could say that Jill is cautious about what she believes. She likes to check people out before she gives them the green light of trust. Unfortunately for her, most of the population seems to be stuck in the red or the yellow, because Jill hardly trusts anybody. She has this amazing gift to discern what is wrong with any church, any teaching, any aspect of the Christian life. So if you need a good "splinter finder" (see Matthew 7:3–5), then Jill is your woman!

If you need someone to evaluate your life, contact Jill. She will size you up quickly and present to you a personal profit and loss sheet. It doesn't matter how self-effacing you are, Jill's figures will be sure to both humble and depress. But enough of the good news. Let's talk about what Jill does wrong.

How Jill Came Tumbling After

Judgmental Jill is almost the exact opposite of Gullible Garfield. She is in the ditch on the other side of the road. If we could just get these two together to learn from one another, the resulting merge would be pretty sound.

I guess Jill's major problem is that she seems unable to appreciate diversity. She is the sort of person who drives to work the same way every day, has the same kind of lunch all the time, and prides herself on having taken her holidays for the last thirty years in the third week of January at What a Boring Beach Resort, only one hundred miles away.

Hasn't discovered that variety is the spice of life

Jill has never discovered that variety is the spice of life and that, as we discussed in chapter one, God is into diversity, especially when it comes to people. A simple look at creation could adequately prove this point. The almost infinite varieties—butterflies and bugs, flora and fauna, peoples and personalities—all point to the fact that, if God used a bank, He would probably have his checks bounced several times due to his lack of ability to sign the same way each time. Jill, however, defines difference as wrong.

I remember listening to a tape of the late David DuPlessis, one of the fathers of the charismatic movement, on his first encounter with Catholic leaders. He was invited to the Vatican to be part of an interdenominational forum. With much trepidation and confessed prejudice, he went expecting heretical devils only to discover that these devils were expecting him to be a raving lunatic. He quickly discovered that he had much in common with those around the table and that his prejudices were fueled more by a lack of knowledge than any guiding, scriptural principles.

If only Jill would spend time and talk with the people she vehemently derides, she would begin to learn they may well have insights into truths that would benefit her and move her toward balance.

Just the other day I received a letter from an Anglican rector who briefly explained that he had been nurtured by the liberal Catholic arm of the church. Based on his background, he had judged our particular congregation as one that must be "narrow-minded, charismatic, funda-mentalist, and arrogant." He went on to say he had been able to hold his views without fear of contradiction because he had never actually met anybody who attended our church. On reading a recent newspaper article about what we believed and the practical impact our church is having on the community, he wrote to apologize for his views and to open the lines of communication. "I quickly discovered," he said, "that we on the liberal side of the church can be as biased and judgmental as those we choose to criticize."

Gnats and Camels

I honestly believe that for many years the church has allowed Scripture's teaching on love, acceptance, and forgiveness to run a dis-tant second place to the value of theological accuracy. Whole ministries devoted to raising the standard of truth between Christianity and other religions have begun to turn their guns on any part of the Christian church they particularly don't like. Unfortunately, much of their comment is ill-advised, one-sided, and, in some instances, mischievous. The majority of such heresy hunting is not about the major doctrines of the church but rather pedantic quibbling and banal obfuscation. (Theological Theo asked me to use this word so that Judgmental Jill will look it up to make sure that it is accurate.)

So the gnat of trivia is strained out, while the camel of division is left floating and decaying. The stench of it all quickly convinces the would-be seeker to continue his quest in more pleasant pastures.

I think the apostle Paul was exasperated over this very point and consequently devoted a good deal of his most important work, the book of Romans, to it. *"Accept him whose faith is weak, without passing judgment on disputable matters"* (Romans 14:1).

"Faith" here is not the individual's personal trust in God. Our friend Frank (chapter six) often has not realized this, especially when he quotes the last part of this same chapter with relish: *"Everything that does not come from faith is sin"* (verse 23). No, faith here is about what one's faith or Christian conviction allows the individual to do or not to do. Examples are given that range from keeping the Sabbath and eating certain foods to drinking wine and other such topics.

Paul said that the church is divided into two groups of people: the strong in faith, those who have freedom of conscience to do many things; and the weak in faith, those whose consciences are more limited in their expression. He did not tell us who is correct but merely stated that the strong should not put the weak down for their lack of liberty and the weak should not condemn the strong for their loose standards. His major point was to major on the majors, to keep the main thing the main thing. Judgmental Jill, however, forsakes the major for the sake of a minor.

Forsakes the major for the sake of a minor

Paul said in Romans 14:5, *"Each* [person] *should be fully convinced in his own mind."* *"Let us stop passing judgment on one another"* (verse 13). *"Let us therefore make every effort to do what leads to peace and to mutual edification"* (verse 19). *"Accept one another, then, just as Christ accepted you"* (Romans 15:7).

Now You're Cooking!

Maybe a good dose of Romans 14 and 15 along with some Ephesians 4 and 5, Romans 12, and Colossians 3; a side order of the entire book of Galatians; and a little bit of 1 Corinthians 13 as a garnish would be the sort of scriptural meal to "unweird" our judgmental friend.

Jill must begin to realize that our standard for Christian living and loving must be taken from the character of Christ—not only from His words but from His actions and attitudes as well.

JUDGMENTAL JILL

- Favorite Scriptures: Leviticus and Deuteronomy 28 (the curses section)

- Least Favorite Scripture: Most of the New Testament

- Gets along well with Theological Theo, as long as he is totally and perfectly theologically sound

- Favorite TV Program: *The People's Court*

- Catchphrase: "It is impossible to be too overzealous when it comes to guarding the truth"

10

PROSPERITY PATRICIA

money speaks, but does it tell the truth?

We have already met one of Patricia's cousins, Frank Faith. The two get on really well, yet Patricia tends to move beyond Frank to concentrate her energy and attention on the specific area of success and prosperity.

More often than not, she will be quick to tell you that the word *prosperous* is a holistic word and includes every dimension of life. Yet watching and listening to her over time shows that, in practice, prosperity and success are defined in terms of net worth, car model, and image.

There's a Whole Lot of Truth Here

Patricia has had her critics over the years. Her fair share of Judgmental Jills have tried to shoot down everything she says, to the point where even the words *success* and *prosperity* have negative connotations. I have noticed, however, that even the guy who writes a book against success wants his book to sell well!

If you think about it, most people want to be successful in life. In fact, I think everyone wants to be. The difference is in the definitions. If you meet someone who wants to be a failure (a rare animal indeed), then the resulting lack of motivation simply means that he will be very successful in achieving his goal, which is failure. So, one is forced into success even when pursuing failure.

What can Patricia teach us? I think, first of all, she makes a very valid point that the words *prosperity*, *success*, and *abundance* are biblical words. Looking at the nature of God, scripturally speaking, one would have to agree that abundance and prosperity are part of who God is. We only have to look at our universe and planet to see that the God who created these did not have a poverty mentality, a barely-get-by view of life. No, our planet speaks loudly of diversity, beauty and abundance. Prior to the fall, the garden of Eden was considered to be very good. Poverty and lack were not part of the picture. Abundance and prosperity were normal to Adam and Eve.

Knows that *prosperity* and *success* are biblical words

Even when we fast-forward through human history and reach the point of the new heavens and the new earth, we find this aspect of God's nature being exhibited. Revelation's account of the New Jerusalem—streets of gold, pearly gates, etc.—is certainly not what we would expect from a deity who thinks lack, need, and poverty are values to embrace. Indeed, we find the exact opposite. If anything, God is guilty of ostentation, going over the top, and being both excessive and extreme.

I am not, of course, saying that this is how Christians must live in our present-day position in the midst of a fallen world. What I am saying is that so often our thinking has been dulled and our viewpoint blinded by excessive preaching on the virtues of poverty.

Blessing or Curse?

If poverty is a blessing, why is it called a curse throughout much of the Old Testament? A simple reading of Deuteronomy 28 should at least bring this truth to our minds. If poverty is a blessing, why does God call us to give to the poor? Why is it that our hearts go out to anyone in need? Why is it that we work and toil so that we can look after our families and put something back into our community? If poverty is a blessing, then we should all try hard to be poor (something that does not take a whole lot of effort) and certainly stop giving to those who are being blessed by God already!

When we begin to look at it in this light, we see that, although poverty might be a regrettable fact of life, it is certainly not life as God designed it. I believe the way to beat poverty is to be solution-minded rather than problem-orientated. Instead of sympathizing with those in need, I believe we should go out of our way to be as successful and prosperous as possible so that we may be blessed in order to be a blessing. So we can give. So we can lend. So we can be part of the solution and not just part of the problem.

The difficulty is, of course, that many Christians just want to be blessed and don't see themselves as conduits for the blessings of God. They become self-centered, greedy, and materialistic, and they use God's Word and their faith for selfish ends. This is not what biblical prosperity is all about.

Lifestyles of the Rich and Redundant

Patricia has got some things right. Where she tends to get into trouble is in the area of priorities. She is so busy believing God for success that she loses the bigger picture of seeking God's kingdom, developing fruit in her own life, and being a herald of the truth of the Gospel to those who are lost.

When she turns to Matthew 6:33, she reads, "Seek first all these things and the kingdom of God will be added to you!" She fails to realize that we are to serve God, not money and the things that money can buy. One only has to speak to those who love money and pursue materialism to find that they lack answers, meaning, and fulfillment in their lives. The search for significance certainly does not lead to the crass accumulation of multiple toys.

Things in themselves are not evil, but when our priorities are out of line, what was designed for good begins to harm us. Patricia, unfortunately, has bought into the old lie of materialism, yet this lie comes in spiritual garb. Bejewelled speakers on the Christian circuit reveal to the willing ear that God wants us

Prosperity
Patricia

to have lots of money. They seem to find this promise in almost every verse of Scripture. More often than not, the way to begin this new journey toward financial independence is to give large sums to the speaker, thus breaking the spirit of poverty over one's own life.

Gets in trouble when it comes to priorities

One speaker I know encourages everyone to bring their bills to a service and, after the offering is taken up, to jump on them, thus demonstrating that debt is broken. As a pastor, one of the things that hurts me the most is that, after the entourage has left town, the majority of these people, sincere and desperately wanting freedom in their financial worlds, continue on, year after year, somehow hoping that God will do a miracle for them. Meanwhile they never change their habits of overspending and neglecting to save money.

I am not saying that God does not move in miraculous ways by helping people find jobs and blessing them with amazing surprises. But the Bible has so much to say about the wise management of finances being a principal key to seeing our needs met and being in a position where we can give and bless others. One message along these lines, if listened to and acted on, would do more good than a hundred sets of so-called "prosperity by believing" tapes. Patricia's problem is that money has become too big in her life. It fills the screen of her consciousness so that God has very little room to maneuver.

You Would Never Guess Who I'm Related To

I might add that there is a variation of Prosperity Patricia, a weird Christian who also allows money to play too big a part in his life, but from a totally different perspective. I am talking here about the sort of person who has made a god out of poverty and lack to the same degree that Patricia has created a god out of material goods and abundance. To this person, the concept of a rich Christian is an oxymoron. (Other examples of oxymorona, for those who are interested, are airline food and council work!)

"Holy people throughout church history have made vows of poverty and have lived minimalist lifestyles," they declare. "In order to deal with poverty in our world, we should empathize, live a simple lifestyle, and try to become as much like the poor as we possibly can." Money consumes their thinking, not as something that is good, but as something that is evil. This is the person who gets upset the moment his pastor begins to speak about giving, money, and tithing. This sort of Christian proves from his reaction that his attitude toward money is wrong. Shakespeare's words apply to this person: Methinks he does protest too much! When anybody speaks about or teaches on money, this weird Christian feels uncomfortable and quickly complains about the overemphasis on the subject.

I'd Love Some Pie!

People who are free to give and happy to do so have clearly shown that their priorities in life are God first and money second. They use their finances to serve their vision and not the other way around. Poverty thinking comes from the viewpoint that there is only so much to go around. Life is seen to be like a pie. If I get a big slice, then someone else has to receive a smaller slice. As a result of this presupposition, negative attitudes, resentment of successful people, and much of the simple lifestyle theology have come to the forefront in our day. In reality, modern economic theory shows that money and wealth in our society are created by diligence, ideas, and actively following dreams. The economic world is not a pie with only so many slices; rather, it is a river that is constantly flowing.

Patricia and her cousin both need to realize that the Bible says a whole lot about money, the importance of giving and receiving, and using wealth responsibly. Patricia especially must not view giving merely as a means to an end—the end being personal, selfish gain. When we give to the local church, to the poor, and to international missions, our primary motive is to bless those in need, help the local church do its work of ministry, and spread the Gospel effectively in other countries.

The act of giving is an act of worship. When we give to get, we worship ourselves, for we have become the primary purpose behind the action.

Following Christ in the area of money management does, however, yield many benefits both for us and for others. God is worshipped, the local church is funded, people are helped, the Gospel is preached, and our own perspectives concerning net worth and true security are challenged. Furthermore, when tough times come, we discover that we become the recipients of God's blessings ourselves.

It is true that a side benefit of normal, generous, no-strings-attached giving is that God begins to get involved in our financial world. Our needs are met as we find ourselves receiving ideas, promotions, and money from unexpected sources. In seeking Him we discover rewards, but in seeking the rewards we can easily lose sight of what really matters.

Prosperity Patricia

PROSPERITY PATRICIA

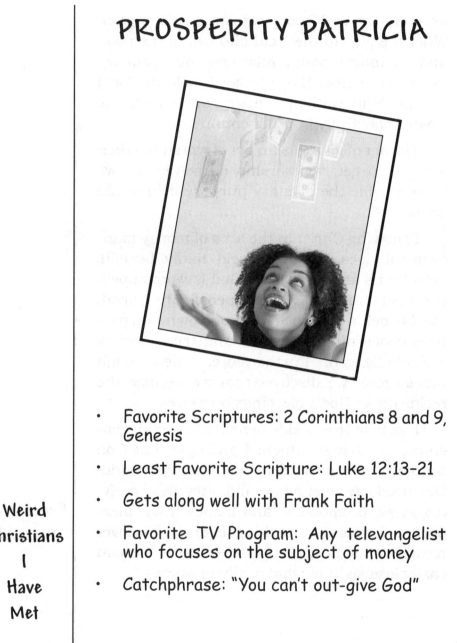

- Favorite Scriptures: 2 Corinthians 8 and 9, Genesis

- Least Favorite Scripture: Luke 12:13–21

- Gets along well with Frank Faith

- Favorite TV Program: Any televangelist who focuses on the subject of money

- Catchphrase: "You can't out-give God"

11

PLASTIC
PETE

if only i could fake authenticity

nauthentic Christianity should be a nonsense phrase. After all, the spirit of Christ is about revelation, honesty, and accepting who we are. Indeed, the primary reason why many people reject the claims of Jesus is that to accept them requires the painful awareness that we are not okay, that we need help. Pantheism declares we are god, but Christianity declares we are fallen and that repentance and faith are our only friends.

So how is it that, for many Christians, honesty and frankness go out the window soon after conversion? Plastic Pete, who should never have been able to survive in the church, finds it to be a wonderful natural environment. Soon our churches contain more Petes, more plastic, and more pretense than professional wrestling. And those who are genuinely seeking God either see through it all and run away or feel there is something wrong with them and sadly move on.

Pete must be stopped. The facade must be broken so that the charade of pretense and denial can come to an end.

Well, Has Pete Got Anything Right?

In short...not a lot. I guess one could argue that his motives are sometimes honorable, although ill-advised. Pete often starts off by wanting to promote what God has done in his life. He then gets the mistaken idea that if God has done anything, He has done everything. Therefore, any suggestion of emotional distress, confusion, fear, or doubt is quickly suppressed. "I must present well," he mutters to himself. "People must not know that my marriage is struggling or that the weaknesses in my life often seem overwhelming." So he smiles on with teeth gritted and pretends, hoping that pretending will grow the fruit of reality if it's given enough time.

Understand this: Most Petes start off this way, not trying to make people think better of them, but trying to make people think better of God. Thus, the weight of the Godhead is on their shoulders. This load can, and will, prove unbearable.

Motives Are Not Enough

Having honorable motivation does not make a thing right. Pete slowly realizes this as the years of false living creep by. This realization, however, does not help. The image is formed and ingrained in his circle of friends and relatives. Too much face would be lost to own up, and so the performance continues, now more for his benefit than for God's.

That's the problem with vicious cycles: They are vicious, and they are cycles. ("That's profound!" I can hear Theo muttering.) The only thing that seems to break this is a real crisis or genuine revelation. Unfortunately, the former is more prevalent than the latter.

Plastic Pete

I think that out of all the weird Christians we have looked at, this one has the greatest potential to harm both himself and those around him. The trouble with pretense is that we lose what is real. The image becomes everything, and the substance seeps out along the way. By the time we realize that everything is wrong, we no longer know what is right. Like a plane without instruments in a storm, the frame of reference is lost, and a crash is almost inevitable. Yet God's truth provides hope, because truth sets us free. But lies only complicate and cloud.

Image becomes everything, and substance is lost

I remember speaking to a friend who had just experienced a blaze of inner light; God's truth on being an authentic believer had burned through years of effort and emotional denial. He had just finished reading *Honest to God?* by Bill Hybels, a book that makes a clarion call to Plastic Petes. Tears ran down his face as he came to grasp that God wants and loves him for who he is. God can take our anger, frustration, and our love. His shoulders are big enough for us. We don't have to jump through a series of religious hoops to sense His smile upon our lives. This is the wonder of Christianity and, of course, the reason why Pete is so out of step, so wrong, so fouled up, and so weird.

A Hostile Environment

One of the compounding problems that Pete faces is that many churches encourage his behavior. Peer pressure or theological persuasion create an atmosphere that is hostile to honesty. Judgment and disapproval fall quickly on those who admit to struggle, and rather than risk social or religious excommunication, Pete stays quiet. This kind of environment goes completely contrary to the biblical ideal of church. The Bible clearly teaches that this new community should be a place where we can *"confess* [our] *sins to each other and pray for each other so that* [we] *may be healed"* (James 5:16).

Surely the community of faith is the one place where we should be able to be honest and receive help and healing rather than condemnation and criticism. The pews and pulpit should not be a natural habitat for inauthenticity. Yet, sadly, for many they are just that.

This idea of "confessing our sins" seems a futile and self-depressing exercise to the outside observer. "Let's not languish in the mire of our own mistakes; let's get on with the job of living." The amazing thing is that God does not share this particular viewpoint. Indeed, the idea of confession is introduced by Scripture as a necessary prerequisite to deliverance.

Many have the mistaken idea that God wants us to confess our sins to make us feel bad, yet nothing could be further from the

Plastic
Pete

truth. God's plan for Plastic Petes is freedom. But freedom can only come from a foundation of honesty and transparency. This truth, one would expect, would be self-evident. Christian counselors and many psychiatrists and psychologists would attest to its veracity. The fact is that we must own the problem, admit to the fault, and confess the sin. Then and only then do we stand the chance of discovering the answers, or the help, necessary to break free.

Pretends everything is okay even when it's not

Denial means we can never receive help, for we do not admit we need it. Alcoholics Anonymous runs on this premise. The declaration, "I am an alcoholic," is absolutely necessary in order to break free from the addictive behavior of the drink-dependent lifestyle. Admitting one has a problem gets us halfway to solving it.

Plastic Petes pretend everything is okay when it's not. They perceive that to admit fault, confess sin, and share problems will only bring intense shame, both from God and from other Christians. Yet God warms to the penitent soul. The humble are warmly embraced by Him. In fact, the first beatitude in Matthew 5:3, *"Blessed are the poor in spirit, for theirs is the kingdom of heaven,"* is all about how God can only move in the life of one who recognizes the need for Him.

The Christian church should also be a place of refuge for those who are struggling—a place where those who confess their sins are encouraged, helped, and loved. We need to salute, not shame, those who are honest enough and big enough to break through the barriers of image and pretense fostered by our culture. If the Plastic Petes of this world will discover that bravado, their cover-ups will be destroyed. It doesn't matter if we are talking about a marriage, a budget, or a self-destroying habit.

Truth sets us free because it releases the power of community and the presence of God into the life of the authentic individual. In short, being plastic takes up far too much energy. Being real may appear riskier, but the rewards are worth the effort it takes to be courageous.

Plastic Pete

PLASTIC PETE

- Favorite Scripture: The entire Bible

- Least Favorite Scripture: Will not admit to disliking any passage

- Gets along well with Frank Faith

- Dislikes Backslidden Bob

- Favorite TV Program: Infomercials

- Catchphrase: "I'm fine"

12.

A
PLEA
FOR
BALANCE

reversing the weirdness

Is there a solution to the weird Christian problem? Is there a way to slow their influence and diminish their numbers?

Using a character-by-character strategy would require much work and energy, as we would find ourselves fighting on multiple fronts. We would have to gather the End-Time Eds and focus our teaching arsenal on practical and authentic Christian living for today. The Demonic Daves would get a dose of the need to resist the flesh while Theological Theos would learn to express themselves by attending the six-day, compulsory, You Are Emotional seminar.

The one thing we all need is balance

No, I think the solution to the weird Christian phenomena is not to try to fight all these small, multiple battles but rather to see what the one thing is that weirdness has in common. What is the shared enemy? I believe, in my study of this subject, the one thing we all need to keep us from straying into the ditches is this thing called *balance*.

If local churches would be fully orbed; if believers across the world were hearing and receiving a well-rounded discussion of Scripture and the Christian life; if teachers taught on faith and sacrifice, rights and responsibility, common sense and spiritual warfare, then, I believe, the number of these weird Christians would begin to diminish.

To Be Balanced or Not to Be Balanced, That Is the Question

The word *balance* does not always receive good press. This is because different people approach the subject from different perspectives. So please forgive my slight embellishment of Hamlet's soliloquy, but I sense many people feel this way when confronted with the subject of balance. Those who embrace the concept with enthusiasm often have in their minds the need for security, keeping away from extremes, or playing it by the book. When we are talking about running a church or running one's life, such a viewpoint has a lot of validity.

Others, however, recoil from the term. To them the word is simply a synonym for boring, traditional, and conservative. These people will be quick to tell you that if you want to get anything done in this world, you have to go out on a limb; sometimes you have to be an extremist. Jesus was hated by the "balanced" religious leaders of the day because he was seen to be extreme.

These comments also have a whole lot of merit. In fact, both the opposers and the proponents of balance seem to have something significant to say. To further complicate matters, it seems that God created us all differently. We are all wired to react in different ways to different situations—one person's balance is another person's extreme.

The first thing we must do is to define our terms. Much misinformation and disagreement on this subject comes about simply by not agreeing upon what the fundamentals of balance actually are.

Biblical balance means that we continue to grow in every area of our lives

Ephesians 3:19 says, *"That* [we] *may be filled with all the fullness of God"* (NKJV). An extreme statement in itself. What I believe the apostle Paul was praying for here is that we, as Christians, would manifest in our lives not just one of the fruits of the Spirit but that we would be suitably matured in all of them. I believe biblical balance means that we continue to grow in every area of our lives, from our relationships to our theology, from our spiritual walk to our physical lifestyle.

Balance is not an equal amount of unbelief and faith, pessimism and optimism, encouragement and discouragement, or good and bad. Neither is it having a chip on each shoulder. No, balance is exhibiting the lifestyle of Christ in every part and dimension of our lives, not in just a few select areas where we allow the Spirit of God to invade. If Jesus is not Lord *of all*, He is not Lord *at all*. A balanced Christian is one who is totally sold out to God in every area.

Probably the subject of balance is best understood if we look at some of the variables, or aspects, of the Christian life in which we are to find equilibrium.

Vertical versus Horizontal

I believe the first area where many Christians seem to get out of kilter is in the balancing of the horizontal. That is, the relationship with God versus the relationship with people. Unfortunately, many see the Christian life simply in terms of their journey with God. They spend time in Bible study and prayer. They go to church as long as it helps them in their connection with Him. And they are quite happy not to get involved in the lives of others. "How is my walk with God?" seems to be the question most asked when judging spiritual growth.

The monastic period in early church history was the logical extension of this kind of lop-sided Christianity. Life was spent in prayer and study, but the truth concerning evangelism, being the salt and light in our culture, and providing input and solutions to many of the problems the world faces was conveniently forgotten. The Desert Fathers may have gained significant revelation on subjects such as solitude, personal discipline, and prayer, but they failed in fulfilling the commission of the church.

Our relationship with God, the vertical aspect of our lives, is of course highly important. Yet it must always be connected to the horizontal. Worship should lead to work, prayer to preaching, and contemplation to community. Jesus never separated the vertical from the horizontal. He talked about loving God with all our heart, soul, and strength, and loving our neighbor as ourselves. Indeed, He even went on to point out that if our relationships with our brothers and sisters, our horizontal walk with people, is not up to par, we have no business coming to God. *"First go and be reconciled to your brother; then come and offer your gift"* (Matthew 5:24).

The Christian life, then, is not just about God, but about people as well. The church is about worshipping God and loving people. From my experience, this second area is the hardest of all. Learning to forgive and receive forgiveness, loving, serving, and encouraging one another is what real Christianity is all about. The horizontal should be the reflection of the vertical within our lives.

Fellowship versus Evangelism

It seems to be very easy for Christians to spend the bulk of their relational time with other members of the body of Christ. We enjoy fellowship with like-minded people. After all, we are part of a new family, a new community, and it's encouraging and mutually beneficial to spend time with people who are heading in the same direction and celebrating the same God. However, God has called us to build relationships with those who are not yet part of the church. The appeal, indeed the command, is to reach out to lost people.

Our impact will only be through contact

Modern statistics on the area of evangelism point out the fact that the most effective way of reaching people is to build significant relationships with them. Jesus, of course, operated this way, much to the chagrin of the Pharisees. He was a friend to sinners and publicans. Jesus was the sort of guy, Tony Campolo would say, "who would throw a birthday party for a prostitute."

I have discovered that many Christians, especially those who have been walking with God for many years, can get out of kilter on this particular variable. They prioritize fellowship over evangelism and schedule all their relational energy toward members of the same body without allowing time for those who are outside the kingdom. The self-absorbed holy huddles that this kind of thinking produces do nothing to further the mission of the church. Our impact will only be through contact. Our time spent with the Christian mechanic and Christian hairdresser may get us cheaper prices, but the kingdom is not advanced. We should not do business only with people who have fish on their car bumpers. We should not pray for job transfers when we find ourselves the only Christians in our places of employment. Thinking this way only means that our faith has become both selfish and second-rate.

When our priorities are out of line, our spirituality will quickly become unfulfilling. One Christian writer used the analogy of sheep dogs. When the dogs spend their time penned together, their energy is expended in fights and snarling. But when they are released to corral the sheep, the bickering turns to delight. They work together, the job gets done, and everyone sleeps better at night.

It is also true that some can get unbalanced in the other direction, where no time is given to fellowship and building Christian community, and truths such as accountability are quickly forgotten. Without these things in the life of the Christian, evangelistic fervor wanes and embryonic Backslidden Bobs begin to take shape.

Truth versus Error

Another continuum on which we must find our midpoint is that of theological balance.

As we have discovered, most error taught in churches or by roving evangelists is not the result of what is said, but what is not said. The exclusion of the other side of the coin is the most common form of heresy.

Teaching on God's mercy and love is right, but excluding all teaching on God's judgment and the legal framework of the universe is a quick path to insipid Christians, impotent churches, lukewarmness, and antinomianism. Teaching on the sovereignty of God, without also covering the importance of our responsibility in life, produces a type of fatalism that destroys Christian endeavor. Teaching on the priority of community, without also teaching on God's love for the individual, can lead to the errors of controlling discipleship and abuse of authority. These errors, and many like them, are more about what is left out than what is covered. The unsaid distorts the said, and the church is deceived.

I believe the best cure for this, in our individual lives and churches, is through the expository teaching of God's Word. Systematically studying the Bible—book by book, chapter by chapter, verse by verse—forces us to deal with passages of Scripture we would normally pass over in the quest for a more exciting promise. End-Time Eds are forced to study the Epistles, Demonic Daves read the book of Romans, and Frank Faiths contemplate 1 Peter. Through such study of God's Word, we discover teaching on subjects such as suffering and victory. We come across the call to social action and corporate worship. We discover the joys of walking in love with one another and the necessity for the correction of God's Word when we go astray.

God looks at the heart first

In short, a book-by-book study of the Bible will promote a balanced theology in that all the experiences, promises, and conditions we find in Scripture are taught and lived out within the life of the church.

Another aspect of theological balance is the search to find the middle ground between information and zeal. Many churches today, in their quest for balance, become pedantic, overly scholastic, and hyper-intellectual in their approach to Scripture. Enthusiasm, zeal, and passion for living are frowned upon.

In my reading of the life of Christ, and indeed the whole Bible, I feel that God looks at the heart first and knowledge second. I know as a pastor I would much rather have a thousand passion-filled, enthusiastic Christians than those who lack fervor but know the implications of Trinity, the hyperstatic union, and one hundred models of church government. If people are keen to pray, believe God, and win their worlds for Christ, they will prove to be far more effective than a thousand graduates from seminary who have their theology together but have lost their joy in the Christian experience.

Joy versus Solemnity

The intense, overly serious, and melancholic individual can often use his or her Christianity to be down in the mouth about everything. Building the kingdom is serious business. We are to be sober-minded, vigilant, and watchful, yet this must be balanced with the call to rejoice.

I am always mindful of the fact that Paul penned the words *"Rejoice in the Lord always. I will say it again: Rejoice!"* (Philippians 4:4) from prison. God never designed the Christian life to be some kind of dirge where morose and thin-lipped believers share their revelations with one another in some valley of sorrow. No, the Christian life is not about pain and sorrow now and joy and fulfillment when we die. The table is prepared in the midst of our enemies. Joy, not grief, is one of the chief characteristics of the God-honoring lifestyle.

I think it is significant that the first miracle Jesus performed was at a wedding party— and what a miracle it was! Jesus provided one thousand bottles of good wine when everyone had already had plenty of choice wine and expected to be served cheap wine for the rest of the evening (John 2:1–11). What did this tell us about the character of God? What does this tell us about the nature of the Christian life? I think, in short, that life is meant to be lived and that Christianity should enhance rather than detract from the pleasures of life. After all, the psalmist wrote, *"At Your right hand are pleasures forevermore"* (Psalm 16:11 NKJV). The misuse of God's gifts leads us astray, but seeking God's kingdom first means you experience more of life, not less of it.

Probably the best biblical example of the balance between sacred solemnity and celebration is found in the book of Nehemiah: *"This day is sacred to our Lord. Do not grieve, for the joy of the LORD is your strength"* (Nehemiah 8:10).

I'm with Theological Theo when he says, "Let's get back to the book of Leviticus!" Levitical Law called for a festival tithe. This was a special offering taken up regularly that, at the end of the year, was designed to be spent in its entirety on a party. This was not money to be given away to those in need or to pay for the new air-conditioning in the auditorium. No, this was money that God's people were meant to spend on themselves. They were commanded by God to blow it all on eating and drinking and being merry. (I can almost hear the shuddering of church treasurers around the world at this thought!)

Why on earth would God make a command about something as non-spiritual as this? I believe it is because God wants us to be balanced. He has nothing against our enjoying life and having fun on the journey that is Christianity.

Those who can laugh in the midst of problems are those who have healthy perspectives. The intense and miserable Pharisee will probably die early of ulcers or pessimism-induced loneliness that drives would-be friends away. Healthy Christians must learn how to balance the sadness with the songs, the pain with the pleasure, and the fun with their faith. Life is about all these things, and God wants us to say, with Tennyson, "live it to the lees." If anybody should be sucking the marrow out of life and seizing the day, it should be those who are walking with their God—experiencing His love, peace, joy, and hope—and whose lives are enriched by genuine Christian community.

In Conclusion...

As you can see from what we have discussed, the word *balance* is a difficult one. It calls upon us to live a first-class Christianity. It does not come cheap, but we enjoy its cost. Balance brings with it everything our hearts have been searching for. The only areas I really struggle over or lack peace about in my life are areas that are not balanced. My prayer for myself, and for all who read this book, is that we journey toward balance, that we grow, and that we are filled with all the fullness of God.

I trust also that if any of our weird Christian friends have read thus far, although they may still have an intense interest in end-times or demonology, they will make the decision to be broader and deeper. Weirdness can be reversed. The process may be slow, but if our intention is to reflect the life of Christ and maintain biblical priorities such as worship, service, and evangelism, then the excitement and fulfillment of "normal Christianity" will be within our grasp.

EPILOGUE

In retrospect, I guess I could have called this book, *Weird Christians I Have Been*. I cannot personally lay claim to each character we have visited, but several of them seem very familiar to me. I guess this is true for most Christians. We are all on a journey, and we can often wander off the road, spinning our tires a little along the gravelly shoulder.

I have visited semi-weirdness on different occasions and dressed in different garb. I was almost an End-Time Ed for a year, and I was a Demonic Dave for several months. I quickly moved on to Frank Faith, Theological Theo and, though I am reluctant to admit it, Backslidden Bob. I will hasten to add that I was always on the fringes of such clubs. But looking back over my Christianity, the route seems to have been characterized by zigzags.

As the years have gone by, my steering has improved. I am able to keep the vehicle on the asphalt and, as a result, my progress has been more consistent. Lurching from side to side has its moments, but it is no way to spend a life, and it certainly does nothing to serve the mission of the church or further a personal walk with God.

The importance of keeping the main things the main things and not giving in to the lure of Christian fads is something, it seems, that only Christian experience and sound biblical teaching can imprint upon our hearts.

So, it's onward and upward, or, as C. S. Lewis would say, "Further on and further in." We need to continue to press forward on the upward way and, as we do so, fix our eyes upon Christ rather than the fascinating side-tracks that seem to lead away from the main road. In so doing, we will be both healthy and balanced, and weirdness will be left in the distance.

ABOUT THE AUTHOR

An international best-selling author, Philip Baker is one of Australia's leading speakers, writers, and pastors. Philip began speaking publicly at the young age of nineteen, and since that time he has appeared before businesspeople, conferences, and churches in most countries around the world, with audiences ranging from fifty people to ten thousand. Philip is both a brilliant communicator who knows his subject and a great entertainer with the ability to combine solid content with humor.

Philip is the senior pastor of Riverview Church, one of Australia's largest churches. He continually works to develop unity with other churches and ministers, which has helped to build a strong Christian network both in Australia and throughout the world.

Philip lives in Perth, Australia, with his wife, Heather. They have three daughters.

Dear God, It's Me Again
Gail Ramsey

We live in a frighteningly fast-paced world—a world that can confuse, overwhelm, and discourage us with its conflicting messages about what really matters in life. With the media's portrayal of unattainable "perfection," the latest health scares, the sad but true stories on the news each night, and the stress of everyday living, it's hard to keep our heads straight—and easy to get depressed. But no matter how alone we feel, God has not abandoned us. He is near, ready to comfort us and give us wisdom for living. In *Dear God, It's Me Again*, Gail Ramsey reminds us that God not only hears our prayers, but He answers them, too. As Gail tackles such questions as "Dear God, how should I cope with this stress?" and "Dear God, how do I handle rejection?" you'll see that He is intimately involved with even the smallest details of your life and ready to bring you victory in any situation.

ISBN: 0-88368-430-6 • Hardcover • 160 pages

www.whitakerhouse.com

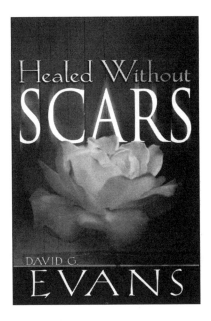

Healed Without Scars
David G. Evans

Have you been hurt by past disappointment, fear, rejection, abandonment, or failure? If so, you've probably learned that time doesn't necessarily heal all wounds. When pain from the past lingers in our lives and causes emotional scars, you need to understand that God is always ready to help you! Discover the path to personal wholeness, and find peace in the midst of life's storms. Renew your hopes and dreams, and experience a life of freedom and joy. For years, author David Evans has helped people from all walks of life learn how to live in victory. Let him guide you to a joyful life of wholeness in Christ as you learn that you can be *Healed Without Scars!*

ISBN: 0-88368-542-6 • Trade • 272 pages

www.whitakerhouse.com

Secrets of Super Achievers
Philip Baker

Have you ever noticed someone who seems to have it all—a great family, financial security, and an adventurous outlook on new challenges? A great life does not happen by accident—it is chosen and requires desire, determination, and faith. Those who refuse to let life happen to them, but instead choose to make life happen, boldly break away from the security of mediocrity and eagerly chase God's best for their lives. Philip Baker provides insight and direction for those seeking to be more than just average and greater than the status quo. He shows readers the secrets to perseverance, balance, focus, endurance, and courage, all with a humor and wisdom that compels and enlightens.

ISBN: 0-88368-806-9 • Hardcover • 192 pages

www.whitakerhouse.com

www.deepercalling.com